The Tongue Has No Bone

poems by

Susan Yanos

Finishing Line Press
Georgetown, Kentucky

The Tongue Has No Bone

ACKNOWLEDGMENTS

I wish to thank the Collegeville Institute for the time and space to create, and the following journals for first publishing some of the poems in this volume:

Presence: "O Come, O Come" and "Second Sunday in Ordinary Time"
The Atrium: "At Fifty I Started Dying," "Stories Told of Me," "Original Grace," "Tide Pool, Laguna Beach"
Saint Katherine Review: "God Who Sent the Dove Sends the Hawk"
Bearings: "Potato Harvest" and "She of Farm I Left Behind"
Frontier Poetry: "Canning Tomatoes" and "The Tongue Has No Bone"

Publisher: Leah Maines
Editor: Christen Kincaid
Cover Art: Katie Trotta
Author Photo: Greg Pyle
Cover Design: Leah Huete

Printed in the USA on acid-free paper.
Order online: www.finishinglinepress.com
also available on amazon.com

Author inquiries and mail orders:
Finishing Line Press
P. O. Box 1626
Georgetown, Kentucky 40324
U. S. A.

Table of Contents

Suffering cannot save, only humility
—Amma Theodora

Those who keep back even a little are torn by devils
—Abba Antony

Your Cell Will Teach You

Saying I do nearly forty
  years ago did not mean I did
  understand my commitment to
a plot of land along with this farmer.

Stay put, the desert *ammas* said,
  be married to your cell.

I learned the rhythm of
  seasons, the priority of field equipment over
  cranky plumbing, the pain of
blisters and bent back. I learned

Long hours in field and kitchen quieted
  mind and tuned ear for
  whimpering babe and stuttering engine
rise in wind.

To do the work, the *ammas* said,
  is grace enough and more.

Demons came, sometimes
  singly or all at once.
Success was the worst, four
  degrees earned over the axles of aging cars;
Then Anger at the paucity of opportunity.

Noon drags in these damned Hoosier
  summers planting, picking, shelling, canning
grading, reading, writing, teaching.
  What's the use? Next year
they are to do again.

Do not judge, the *ammas* said,
  let it bake out of you.

In smoke and tears, how deeply that

root thrusts, I fear when it breaks
loose and slides shriveled to the compost heap
what's left will be a blackened husk.

I ask, who was that young bride?
  I ask, who am I now?

Today my husband called just to say
  fourteen cranes huddled in broken
  cornstalks of the east field
caught by an early spring snow.

As he talks I see them, white
  on white, staying put until
  Sun entices them upward flying
free. I thirst to join them.

Note: During the 4th C., women and men from all classes and occupations abandoned worldly pursuits to live in desert dwellings, or "cells," forming the first monastic communities. They became known as *ammas* (for "mothers," especially a spiritual mother) and *abbas* (for "fathers"). Pilgrims would seek them out, asking for a word. Their sayings can be found in Benedicta Ward's *The Sayings of the Desert Fathers* (Gethsemani KY: Cistercian Publications, 1975).

O Come, O Come

They say the transition at midlife
is something like a third birth:
the first from womb to light, the
second from child to might, and
now this one, not long before night.

My first I barely remember, except
for being scared—of pain, the hospital,
what she would look like, becoming
a mother. A purple fruit she was, ripe
just as harvest began, smelling of
sweet clusters from sun-blessed vines.

The second did not catch me so
unaware. She grew rapidly as the days
grew short. Scared no more, I paced the
house, weight heavy upon me. Cramps ate
across my back. Nights of heartburn marked
an advent calendar of my own, until she
slipped into the snowy stillness of solstice.

This third has gone so long I'm worn
nearly passive, afraid heart and lungs
will give out, too soon, not soon enough.
A wrinkled monster she must be now,
swimming in dark waters oblivious
to the midwife's due date, awaiting the call
from one she will recognize. I pound my
belly, kick furniture, weep.

At Fifty I Started Dying

First to go was the brown in my hair. Second
the womb—a major trauma that; then the
creaking knee, the sagging chin. Let beauty die

my mother complained at fifty when she was flabby, drab
and angry. At seventy she's stunning—halo of white, thin
from oral surgery, outgoing since widowed. Quite the makeover

suffering, but I fear I lack my mother's phoenix genes,
resembling more my father who died little by little after losing
his business until finally I took what was left

and put it in the grave. They say daughters without
fathers jump into promiscuity. As I stand before the
the self in the mirror, still grieving, I pray that's true.

You Grew Up Doused in Blood

You grew up doused in blood:
   the slit throats of the cattle
   your father slaughtered there
   on the cold killing floor.
The barrels of offal streaked
   with red ooze
   drawing flies out on the back landing.
You carried vials of blood to school
   for your classmates to examine under the scope,
   even a vial of your father's blood.
He held his finger, severed at the tip,
   over the jar you'd left for him to
   collect some sample
   before he had the doctor sew back the flesh.
You yourself leaked gallons of it
   so heavy each month you became anemic
   and went under the surgeon's knife.
So why the white face now, the clouded mind,
   the inability to gather the things needed
   to staunch this flow?
My sock clings soaked,
   my foot sloshes in my workboot.
My leg, your hands, my pain, your panic
   stitched together in my silky, bright blood.

Spring in Tornado Alley

April can indeed be cruel
for despite the Lenten fast
cold-rooms ring hollow as empty
Ball glass reflects the bare
bulb's light. We plant seeds,
our bellies gnawing, and pray.

Palm Sunday the sky turns green
and we drag blankets, lanterns,
children to dank basements,
the fronds of our morning hosannas
left on the table. Later we drive past
flattened farmsteads and offer our blood.

We know the places the corpses
are buried, just watch where
green fingers of hosta rise from
the sodden ground. During Triduum
trillium bloom, their erect stalks crowned
with a single bud the color of dried flesh.

In the grass come Easter morn blue
eggs lie chilling, pushed from spruce
by mockingbird who steals
both nest and song. The hearts
of our snowbirds return to fields
left fallow and family untended.

This is the month that tests our
faith, this the month that tests;
we gather at elevator and diner
and tell our tales of wind
outlasted and the last
unwinding of hope.

Planting Seedlings

Someone once praised Voltaire
for the work he'd done for posterity. Yes,
he agreed, he had planted four thousand trees.

Yesterday I left my books to help plant an acre
of trees—East Anglia Scotch, White Spruce,
Southwestern Pine—destined for future Christmas morns.

We paid our teen-aged neighbors to sit the transplanter,
shoving feathery seedlings into furrows, the
angled wheels behind closing soil on roots.

My husband guided the Deere across
the field. I tramped behind, spade over my
shoulder, to replant their mistakes.

Rarely looking up, I knew where I was only when
my feet crushed sod at fence line or waterway. Knob and valley
became one beneath, cloud and sky melded into drizzling rain above.

Occasionally a killdeer screamed, a bobwhite called
from the scrub at the rig far ahead. I picked up another
orphaned seedling and tamped it in.

God Who Sent the Dove Sends the Hawk

From the kitchen window I watch as
doves waddle clown-like round puddles of corn
spilled near the grain pit, then fly into vents
gaping on bins, or from guy wire to wire
like trapeze artists with toes reaching sure
for lines stretched taut from grain leg to the ground.
No net below.

As I go about my chores, I hear them
inside the bins, invisible feathers
whispering against metal walls. When I
straighten from pulling weeds in the garden, mind
elsewhere, their cooing warbles me back: dirt
smudged on knees, green juice staining fingertips,
sweat at hairline.

Sometimes they wheel above barns and house, gray
discs in the sun. Flying rats, our hand mutters, and begs
to shoot at them, tired of smeared windshields and
levers. This year an albino has bred
white under dusty plumage of its kin.
Over our farm's endless browns and dull greens,
their beauty wings.

They were the first to die after the hawk
moved in. Our black-and-tan found a carcass
in the yard and brought it to the back door, bloodied
white feathers fringing her mouth. Yesterday
I found another near the chicken coop,
eyeless. I check the latch before I leave,
scanning the sky.

Now no birds clown round the grain pit nor coo
from the wires. Feeders near windows sit full;
suet cakes hang whole in the lilacs since all
finches and cardinals abandoned us. I
must do my chores with no feather to change

my sight, wondering why it is I fed
doves, drawing hawk.

Today a shape appeared in the lilac's
belly: a bag blown in by night, I thought,
or rotted garbage. But it turned, revealing
beak hooked and smooth, and looked at me. Though I
looked hard, I could not see beyond those eyes.
Not moving, its talons gut my tamed truths,
expose my soul.

Strawberry Picking

First season we were open
I lost ten pounds in two weeks
crawling, cramped, from sun-up on
between green mounds dripping dew.
I cradled a berry in each palm, stems
between thumb and finger to break,
not bruise.
Two hundred boxes a day.
My arms and face burned raw,
mind numb from dehydration,
at sun-down, I cooked meals
still wearing a hat and long sleeved shirt.
Then later in bed,
my skin peeling off in layers,
I picked berries all night
back bent
in my dreams.

Death on the Farm

You can name the pups, of course,
the cats and laying hens, milk cows,
but not those intended for the freezer.
4-H auctions are particularly hard, watching
ten year olds let go a reserve champion they've trained
to show, rump hair brushed and hoofs shined clean,
to some small town butcher with the highest bid,
greedy to get his picture in the paper.
You get used to it after years although
the half-deaf dog caught under the tractor wheel
still pulls a bit as you watch the viburnum
blossom over its grave. But you prepare as you can
for what you know is coming.
What you do not know is how you'll act
when Ruffian thrashes against your chest
as you cinch the bag tighter around his head.
Mercy is stopping the hours of seizures
caused by worms gnawing his brain
from living with raccoons before you
tamed and loved him.
Perhaps. Or perhaps mercy
is to embrace all, even yourself.

Canning Tomatoes

Arms tired from grinding the handle
I exert what I can to scrape flesh
from skin which then rolls
into flaked tubes chasing the blades
of the mill. So much of my life spent
on food. Juice sieves from grate, a good
measure, pressed down, shaken, overflowing
the bowl in the sink. I stop and empty
into pot on stove. On other burners,
quartered sections boil down and the canner
heats. Jars and rings wait in sudsy
water. Steam fogs kitchen windows, blurring
outside from in, in from out. More
buckets of late-picked fruit
sit at the kitchen door.

The mill and heat do the work yet
much preparation is required. It
wasn't enough to cut open; I had
to boil, crush, season with thyme,
simmer. In the months ahead,
I will serve him, poured out over
pasta, sopping into crust, or holding
beans in chili. Red pulp mingles with sweat
staining my arms, cloths discarded
on counter, drips from elbows, smears
across gut. I turn back
to the mill. Just then he comes,
smelling of ripe grain, and enfolds
me from behind, his scar-pocked
hands plating my breasts.

Recessional, Abbey Church

Visiting, I know not the hymn yet
struggle through the unfamiliar rise

and fall of sound, the sense all
but lost. Melody hides within organ's

reverberating chords, filling space, pushing
away all but husband's familiar voice sure

and strong mapping its own way. He can't
read music, reads himself, wrong. By now I've

lost my place. They begin the third verse.
I turn ear inward. Only what is lost can

be found: my own voice rarely true,
untrained, unable to find pitch.   Not to be

trusted, comes a whisper. And the choir
room's piano tinkles from shadows, benched

as I was at its chipped keys because altos
complained my voice led them

astray. Deeper still I listen, fulfilling love's
first duty and dare to lose and lose again.

A Parable of Prodigality

He wants me to write him a check, our hand, standing
outside the kitchen door, skinny, pale and reeking
of tobacco. Divorced with a common-law wife.
Alcoholic, recovered. Working poor. Liar.

He lies now. I've been warned not to do or if I
do, make it small, not what he asks. It's up to me
so I was told. If it were up to me I'd fire
his skinny ass for days not worked, tools gone missing.

Ingratitude. But we don't. We can't. It's not up
to me it seems. Not since he started asking for
the future paid out now, the present want plainly
pain. I fill blanks with no more than the sums I'm told.

After all this time, even now, I ask not for
an accounting, try not to judge one who prays to
the god of benevolent lotteries for at
the end I hope for luck to slyly wink at me.

I'm taking too long, I know, angry he's waited
until I'm alone to knock on my door while my cats
sniff his pant legs in recognition. Someone must
have chalked a summons to vagabonds on corner post.

A soft heart. They have that right at least. It's softness
that shrinks from both polarity's clang and virtue's
claim. Having failed the moment I'm now bound to see
this through. He coughs outside and I pick up the pen.

Dry Summer

Frogs stopped singing weeks ago, their creek bed
cracked. We walk where we could not walk before,
finding burrows dug by beavers empty
now and exposed along the banks. Red tail
hawks arc above tractor and sickle bar,
watching for rabbits flushed from timothy.
When none run, they turn screaming on themselves.
Wind, ceaseless wind, curls impatiens, bleaches
grass, flaps cottonwoods into joyless song.
At home, for daily discipline, I lug
five-gallon water pails to trenches dug
in garden, trusting leaves will open still,
as the old monks I'd read commanded. Yet
tomatoes turn tough and hard seeded. When
I lift yams like bulbous hands from their hills,
they bear the stigmata from feeding mice.
Coyotes move in closer. Out past dark
I hear them in the barnlot. Something wild
in me croons back: another sleepless night.
By day dust shrouds combines, its wan fingers
embracing road and field and man alike
and reaching into hot engines to spark.
I see smoke in the distance, drive by our
neighbor's blackened machine, relieved it is
not ours. On the way back through lands now reaped,
I climb out often, sniff the air, then just
to be sure, get on my knees, palms flat on ground,
and check the underbelly of the truck
for stalks lodged near the heat; fatigue and fear
contending mates who faithlessly whisper
wind-tossed petitions not answered, not heard.

First Frost

They always get it wrong, city forecasts
covering outlying space, and I forget
to doubt and drag out heavy tarps in case

so morning finds my garden ruined. What
I'd planned to shield—tomatoes, melons—gone
to mush. White crystals smother lawn and field

stubble. I stand at my plot's edge, palming
the egg I gathered just before, still warm
brown, flecked with blood. I'm tempted to deplore

all lost. Yet deep within something quickens
that throughout summer's heat had slumbered as
fat insects thrummed a wild relentless beat

abruptly stilled. Into this strange silence
I lean not to end but begin hearing
something which pulses beneath thatch of what's been.

Driving Home from School

My sister wants to buy a house near town
trading the expanse of snowy field and pasture

for convenience of neighboring store and school.
But I tell her of grace which miles in car

can bring, with daughter yet undistracted by sums
to add and plates to wipe, ready to unroll

the length of day and mind and heart
if I am but still. As the wheels rock us

into dusk past cows trudging with bloated udders
toward supper and stanchion, this skittish

one beside me eases from the silence, lets down
her words, and I ride into her soul's vast acres.

Second Sunday in Ordinary Time

Awaking to a snow-muffled
farm, the morning so sharp
the very house timbers sing
out, my body sags into a litany
of single digits and layers
of clothes, hot water to carry,
time eaten by chores.

Breath rings against the steely
air and sunlight pings from barn
eaves edged by icicles, then crashes
onto glazed hinges and troughs
I must free of ice, steam sighing
from pail to incense my head
bowed, hoary cap pulled low.

Around the stumps of cornstalks,
mouse tracks skitter, calling
where fallen kernels lie, but I turn
away, pulled to stillness before
the mock orange which flutters
with red and black feathered forms,
its bare branches crackling, unconsumed.

Out of Oil

Nearly midnight, I awake to find the bed cold
and his side empty. I run through my litany of disasters:
children not breathing, house violated, barn afire, cattle out.

I listen. Naught but the wind rattling the windows.
Nothing else, not the whoosh of a toilet nor whir of
the furnace fan. I stretch one arm into the dark.

Down in the basement, my husband clanks metal
doors. His voice rises up the stairs, sharp and cold.
I bring him another flashlight, newspaper.

I find him hunched over the wood stove
he built five years ago but which we'd abandoned
for the new furnace, now standing silent.

The place reeks of oil—although I learn from his grunted
replies there isn't any in the tank—and damp
concrete, kraut fermenting in the crock.

A sulfurous smell, then paper alight, the bluish flame
reflecting in the jars of tomatoes and pears put up
against want, their rubber seals but thin protection.

The tinder catches, pops. I watch his shadow writhe
on the glowing wall behind, then gather my robe
around chilled ankles, climb the rough-cut steps.

Back in bed, I listen to the roar of creosote burning
in the chimney, knowing house and barns are cardstock
against February's onslaught, a family a doorstop before oblivion.

My War with Mink

I mark the unnatural glint in its eye,
the dark pelt muffling the throat
of the old bird; and once again
I'm a child in church gawking
at the woman ahead in communion
line, ignoring the presence offered
by priest. I open my eyes to what's
left of my flock before me now,
feathers black and red, soft and supple
beneath my hand as if still alive.

Longing to kill as it has killed
I set some traps in the coop
then fork in clean straw, patch
wire, bury the dead, add the bait.
But the three survivors who watch
all will not leave the perch
nor burden laid on me. I must
find them a different abode.
Weeks pass before they lay again.

Driving home near dusk, I'm startled
by a lean long shape streaking across
the road, so fast it may just be imagined
and not real presence slipping
formlessly between light and shade,
solid and space. No hand-built
coop can bar this thing, whole as it
is. For a moment, heart quickens,
eye opens, mind stops. It's one.
Once home, I check my traps.

I Lay with My Husband

When my father died, my grief a
demanding lover, I lay with my husband
counted his heartbeats and wondered
when would I enter the desert
with my widowed mother,
when a combine crush,
an auger bite, a bin collapse.

I thought, watching deserted wives, that
it would be as if I had been thrown
upon his fiery pier, wrapped
in a sari of despair.

I laid up preparations against
the years of solitude, learned
to install furnace filters, cock a gun,
tighten a leaky faucet, select a
watermelon against the thump of
my own over-ripe chest rather than
the thump of his, sweet and crisp.

But enter barren land with no guide!
How to rent the farm? give
my daughters in marriage? I tried
to ward off pain by needing him less.

I took trips by myself—a day, several
days—to see how it felt
to sit in a restaurant, plates before me,
alone. Does one read, stare at one's plate,
watch the other diners?
And I found
I could live without him.

Not having chosen our home
nor geography, I asked
did I prefer a cabin in the woods,

a Victorian in a small town?

Less his image grew, as I toyed with
shaping my life around
my will, not ours. I could have
the fireplace I wanted, more
closet space. Why wait? I cleaned
bricks, mixed concrete, made a room of my own.
I found I could live.

One evening, he entered my room,
smelling of rain-soaked furrows, a guest
and stranger. I lay with him, rose
and fell to the dance of his heart,
mine aflame on the altar of his chest.
From the ashes: other, vows, love
I found.

Aftermath

After my father-in-law lay down on the floor
and set a shotgun to his chest, after his boys spat out
what he'd dished in until we all tasted it again

after they returned to the combines for not even
that could halt harvest, after we saw him mounded
over in a treeless corner stolen from a field

my husband and I to replace what was ruined
selected carpet dull enough not to be noticed thinking
we wouldn't see and have to do what comes after.

Prayer for the Heart

Something is wrong within my aging heart.
It jumps and flutters like a struggling bird
with a weight on spindly legs it cannot part.
It frightens me: this free thing I've fettered.
I took their tests to hear what I already knew.
They feed me iron, cut life-bearing sites
away, assured they've staunched tissue
and anemic flow of electrolytes.
But the frail bird flits still. I do not tell
them we have failed. I do not confess. Such
measures leave me a crone not wise nor well.
Scars leaden, angers surge: I mourn too much.
Bitterness, great burden for age to part.
Create in me, O God, a weightless heart.

Upon Turning Sixty in October

Unless you be born again . . .   *(John 3:3)*

Do not ask this—howling winter
soon bearing down—this just now do
not ask:

born in ripeness to reject nectar
of pear, hanging heavy from bough, for rhubarb's
tart spikes

abandon sanctuary padded with costly
harvests for road of endless summits and wind
tormented tent

let cold locked in bones seep into flesh
and brain until it under scalding sun
boils dry.

Too much your call too
much I fear I must say no while do
yes.

Becoming Silence

I would like to talk to the woman who has forgotten words
who discovers new relationships each day
as she encounters again names for what she has known
who thinks the corners of triangles taste like rhubarb
because they both prick the tongue.

I would like to talk to the woman who regards words as rabbit traps
which once the rabbit is caught
can be stored away in a cobwebbed shed, forgotten
who is not trapped herself into a single stop between
future reaching to past through present.

I would like to talk to the woman who can delight
in the sound of bimbo, fuck, weak
the way lips pop or breath hisses, throat contracts
without remembering the men who choked her opinions
obliterated her experience with words become weapons.

Oh the wounding she remembers
a wordless, soundless thing like soil cracking before seedling
or clods broken by rain. Germination, erosion—yes, like that
a yielding to sibilants
like silence, like that.

I would like to share the speech of silence with the woman like that.

She of Farm I Left Behind

So I have boarded barque and sailed
the roads to monastery; left
my hens in others' care to play
at being monk awhile. No world
for women this but woman I
have left behind, in search—of what?
of bliss? Conveying journals blank,
some coin, and only what could fit
in trunk, I traded rustic cell
for one of century-cured brick where
good few before have lived and died,
broke vow of marriage bed with ease
for pallet chaste—these winter months
at least. Obedient to voice
I cannot name as ill or kind
I practice discipline tried by some
with pen and page. Pileated
woodpecker rings matins and I
come hooded, muffed, from fire to walk
glazed trails through wood and cloister dark.
Silent my days, and still the nights
except for visitations by
what I trust is owl perched on roof,
drawn by mice skittering between walls
or what goes skittering in my brain.
It hunts through dreams where nothing's safe
from flaying beak, not even hopes
I hid so well I can't recall
myself. But there they are next day
in scat it's strewn on pages—bits
of hair and bone I recognize
belong to me. They work their way
in lines until I draw curtains,
stoke fire, avoid window and strain
for word I came in hope to hear.

Silence Conquers Any Trial

Awaking as I do in the dark
before dawn my night callers scuttle
from me like roaches to hide
beneath bureau until light
again snaps off. Their fusty smell
lingers. For a moment I forget
where I am and as any other
nocturnal inmate orient sense
to space behind my curled back.
But he is not bedded here with me
because I am not there. My desire
pulled between poles of longing and
satiation knows not how it can endure this
pendency. Absence becomes palpable
presence signified by no word
his name not even a whisper
on my lips. I hunger for home yet
thirst for what will if I stay
until night is through if
I can. Scuttling starts up once
more from some corner dark.

Adrift in a Keel-less Boat

Once pockmarked by glaciers, this land which birthed me
floats above caverns of antediluvian waters still fed by rivers
lost into fissures: a hidden sea which threatens to rise.

For decades I foolishly tread through grassy waves sure
of foot, sure words held Word as the same clouds skate
across sky and lake, until a sinkhole swallowed me whole.

Now I find myself adrift in a keel-less boat within a vast
amnion of fluid dark and coldly indifferent, without oar,
without sail, like some Irish votary doing penance.

I should have been better prepared. Had I not seen
that a dog drinking from stream laps up itself?
that cattails nod serenely to their enchained twins?

Although no wind stirs up whitecaps, my currach rises
and falls as eyeless Leviathan, that plaything of Chaos,
swims beneath. Water heaves inboard. Mother, steady me.

Clinging to gunwales, I stretch for glimpse of depth and see
myself. Sometimes by indirection one finds direction.
I stir the waters with outstretched finger and look again.

Awakenings

I think it all comes down to this:
What is asleep must awaken

I think of fairytale teens suffering a stranger's kiss
dragons robbed of their corrupting hoard
a daughter believed dead commanded arise

I think

You cannot live
in wasteland seared by dragon snoring
nor thicket strangling beauty on her bower

Both lands must be pillaged by hero
or wayfarer, beloved
or thief

I think

In awakening the one within I have disturbed
the other. Now they must be dealt with but
will feeding one nourish two, slaying one destroy both?

That's the riddle I must solve to stay alive
I think.

Original Grace

A landlocked child, I dream of oceans—
continental basins cradling leviathan
and manatees disguised as mermaids—

falling awake while murmuring a creed
of coelocanth, crustacean, barnacle, anemone.
Claws and tentacles stretch for alms

cast from the dinner of others: a descending incense
of salty spray and rotting flesh summoning
sightless ghastly things from depths

intriguing, and terrifying. So much life
and life from death occupying
every crag. Even but a drop a small globe

unto itself inhabited by millions of spawn
and diatoms rocked all night on waves
pulled by a transcendent moon.

Stories Told of Me

a toddler of unbroken eggs:

baby sister fussing—Mother's attention
elsewhere—I rolled her from the bed
stacked round by pillows, and cradled her
to the kitchen, Mother afraid I'd drop,
I'd trip, bones to break.
Yet I carried her safely as I carry her now
with stories of things

I don't remember

learning by heart ad jingles
taught by my cousins to serenade visitors,
or offering Uncle Red and Aunt Claro a beer
cold from the fridge, then trying the lock
on the bathroom door.
The firetruck came red and loud with ladder
to climb through, get me out the window
opened myself onto the green yard

I don't remember

the small plastic pool in the grass
of the rented house once home
to General Meredith, a boxy brick mansion
divided into apartments full of antiques,
cooking smells, and history not mine.
Wet panties my only suit against
the diving beetles, I stripped them off,
ran nude through spaces

I don't remember

what became of this daring child
as rubbed from remembrance
as the fur from the stuffed bunny

she loved bare and eyeless
that Dad kept against careening time
until time cradled him into timeless memory.
Can she carry me, too

with stories I remember?

Piano Recital

No bashful fairies tiptoed through light-daubed
arpeggios in our memorized piece,
nor mountain kings rolled rocks from towers steep,
echoed down crags by pedal-damping chord.

And yet she glided through duets with us
as if it did not matter the swift bark
she piloted, by metronome's scribed arc,
carried within its hold pitch-sealed such

disharmonizing crews to parents' much
relieved applause. She then entrusted each
with crystal cup of scarlet punch to nest
on plate which wobbled greatly as it perched

on Sunday petticoats and clip-on ties.
Munched cookies crumbled on her polished floors
as all us kids of farm and small-town stores
squirmed under critical parental eyes.

We gazed round rooms adorned with walls
of books, prints other than Jesus at prayer,
and sculptures we did not dare touch. Upstairs
a ballroom, whispered one. A room meant all

for dancing! We could barely just believe.
But anything seemed possible in a home
where a pagoda stood on rolling loam,
impractical but for the view achieved.

Forgotten her commands to mind the flat
and fingering at our lessons each week.
Forgotten practice at pianos cheap
where wedged between the couch and chair we sat,

the day's work meted out in half hour ticks
of kitchen timer often checked to see

if slave to keyboard or finally free.
Party now over, we gathered our things.

No longer tethered by black marks on page
to wordless tunes, fancy flies o'er octaves
to spy pixies peeping from cupboards' gloom,
a swish of king's cloak as he leaves the room.

An Afternoon at Grandmother's

In the house with no doors we walked
on tiptoe across carpeted floorboards
to keep from rattling china in the corner cupboard

while she napped upright in her chair
we read old Sad Sack comics with pages
missing or studied photographs lining the ledge—

a grandfather we never knew, a much younger father—
tried to match twenty three cousins with uncles and aunt
and waited for the cuckoo to emerge from its door

later with her arms slathered in pink lotion
from pulling poison ivy from peonies, she served us
buttered toast thickly dusted with powdered sugar.

Bad Karma, Too Many Have Said

To grow up next a slaughterhouse
and cemetery, cutting ruts
in brain and bone, or so others

explain my brother's haunted days
of vein-throbbing dark. But I think
such haunts explain my love of shrouds:

Dad, wrapped in dark one still as death,
lunged wild from gravestones Hallows eve
while we kids still as birth sucked breath

and shrieked at life. Or gray ones split
wide from which milkweed's seeds arise
haloed in white. For them I climbed

barbed wire near chicory, Queen Anne's
lace, careful not to tread on tombs.
Once gilded, trimmed with felt and beads

they hung from limbs we wound with lamps
come Christmas. Skins of Mayfly nymphs,
black walnut hulls that stain the walk,

or fluid sheathed embryos killed
when Dad butchered sows. He laid them
in my hand, commas of ridged spine

marking the luck all mammals share
in evolution's game of chance
and fate. The pigs preserved in jars,

I took them to the science fair
where kids gawked as if I'd brought freaks.
Or now these shrouds I seam myself,

from remnants of memory lean

and false, then drag near rotting biers
to bag weathered bones I've picked clean.

In the Room We Once Shared

Remember, Sis, the twin hot water bottles
in our one big bed, the trouble

to place them just right to keep
toes warm until sleep but not shock

us awake when we uncurled from spooning
before morning light. We wore the same

pajamas but in different colors just as
at Christmas we got the same dolls, mine

brown-haired like me, yours blond
like you. Remember, lights out,

how we traced letters on each other's skin
like code, reaching under night shirt,

our backs slates easily erased
when done—something I did with my own

young girls, sitting so still while deciphering
stroke and dot. I wonder if you did

the same with yours. You threw yourself about
in sleep. I woke with you on top, breath whispering

in my ear. Whatever message came from your
dreams I did not understand or was it that you

did not tell, as you did not when your marriage
bed rumpled. Aggravated, I pushed you away.

Was that it then? Or was it when I convinced
Dad we needed two beds or when you won

fair ribbons I coveted; when I set expectations

at school under which you chafed; when you complained

you had to live in my shadow. Because you
lived there, I found something's hidden,

even from me. Hidden, too, are the veins
that bind. The same salts I inherited flow through

me as they flow through you. My blood
thickens: do you weep?

The *Camino*

Packing the last of it, I stand
next the empty house. Dad
gone, his locker plant burned,
both lying beneath grassy mound.

Mother now gone too. Naught remains.
Not the school I biked to, basket
filled with vanilla, butter, eggs,
practicing my 4-H project.

Not widow lady E—, her gift
of Popsicles compensating
Sister and me—but just a bit—
for an hour's piano playing.

As we rode home we stuck out our
tongues orange and green at each other,
even at our absent mother
for making us visit this neighbor

missing her own grandchildren. Not
the bridge I leaned the bike against
finding shells when crawdads I sought.
Myself a marine biologist

I dreamed, and prayed this road would lead
to oceans vast and unexplored;
not the house of hidden rage where
the new boy moved in—coal black hair

gray blue eyes beneath sleepy lids.
Not even the pink bike that began
our courtship, which he said should hang
on the wall above our shared bed.

It too is gone, stolen from the rack
outside my dorm those years ago.

Only the road—pointing to what I lack
and to what I have yet to do

before light ends and bats descend.
I turn my burdened car to head
down this county road. Dust ascends
like guiding stars as west I bend.

Tide Pool, Laguna Beach

A child once more, I join two women
who strangers though they are

point to what had been hidden:
fat stars glittering in dark crevices,

hermit crabs at war. Delighting at
the slimy grossness of slugs, the seductive

dance of anemones, I am soon bored,
wanting more, goaded by things

read and imagined. The bottom veiled
by bending light, we three crooked like

witches on rocky wasteland
decipher fates in the constellations

of purple urchins rimming the watery world,
eyes averted from the oncoming tide.

Looking Back

I see her in the rearview mirror
legs pumping hard

as her clunky pink bicycle
attacks the incline on 700 South.

Her face tugs at memories
so deep they flit from light

like the name of an old classmate
encountered unexpectedly at county fair

flits from my tongue's tip.
She's determined to get

where she's going. We
both are. I crown the hill

and lose her.

When Sarah Followed

When he brought me to the farm
soiled diapers left by earlier tenants
spilled from the chicken coop, the roof
of the back shed lay in rubble on the floor.

The barn is sound, he said, though too
low for any tractor. We walked to what
remained of the yard and orchard,
dead peach trees marking a grim sentinel.

On the back porch, rat holes the size
of open mouths gaped at me; inside
blackened grease clung to the kitchen
ceiling, plastic bandage strips covered

chips in walls, the wooden floors
ruined by dog piss. I knew I had
to make a choice: laugh or cry.
He watched for my reaction.

With faith in his faith, I abandoned
my ways and stepped into
this marriage, learning a new
vocabulary along with customs,

making picnics of meals hauled
to fields, meditations of commutes
to my classes, virtues of buying
cheap and doing without. I dreamed

of shrub roses where giant ragweed stood,
of a white-clapboard house cooled by
long-limbed trees, a porch where we
could watch the rain roll in, a study

lined with books, dark-haired children
hanging upside down from peach trees

laden with pale blossoms. I used
to wake myself with laughter.

When Sarah Laughed

The drought of '88 tested him.
His worry clouded as cloudless
days stretched before us, the corn
leaves blistering, spider mites

infesting the beans. I took on more
off-farm work to pay the bills. September
proved his worry groundless. The wagons
came in lighter, yes, but prices soared.

He faced the new year sobered but
rewarded. I bowed under my load.
This covenant with land is not
mine and now that I am old, barren,

what can I birth? I laugh
to myself, noting the sound
that springs from a hope long
suffered mimics incredulity.

Preaching Your Cousin's Funeral

Do you speak of anger
  two kids still in school
      and debt their inheritance
so self absorbed
  the body for her to find
      when she got off the night shift
      dog barking at the crushed grass
he abandoned them, abandoned you
  stuck with this task
      because he had no pastor
      to do it for us

Do you speak of horror
  my God face half gone
      the wailing at the funeral home
your aunt cradling him
  there
  on the slab
  against all advice
      before cremation
      the drape sliding off
my God

Do you speak of fear
  a poet—like you
      but he made his rhyme
      sang them to an electric guitar
one last left for her to find
  a weak heart—like you
      but the fault in yours
      is deeper than biology
is there a room in the mansion
  for one like him
  one like you

Do you speak of guilt
  that which we don't take on

and that which we do
            but shouldn't
they come for absolution
    for failing to hear
    in his voice that night
            a tone different
            a word off key
    playing the saved message over
            again
forgive him forgive them
    they don't know what to do

Do you speak of despair
            beyond all, beyond reach
    denied disability
            a leech on her paycheck
    visited by ghosts
            father dead abusive stepfather
    haunted by genes corrupted and passed
            to him
            through him

Do you speak of love
    trite that word
you select his photo for the program
    embrace her you barely know
    watch your cousins as they arrive
    lost and hungry for the jobs you give them
            order at printer's
            finding more chairs
you sit on your aunt's spare bed writing
            rewriting
    while she smokes another pack on the patio
can love hold all this
such tiny things
    to breach the distance
            words

At the Hour of Compline

The maw of night yawns lazily and I
fascinated before it stare in spite
of myself. Not so frightening after
all, a bit bewitching really: moisture
tipped lips, a plump tongue slipped in dusky folds
of throat. I could just slip there too, lie curled
against day's endless chores and yield

and in yielding forget I am. No more
to sing of wounds and drought, lost dreams which sour
what's left if met unsung, their spell released.
No more to mark the snowdrop's slow progress
toward spring, soybeans rolling in ribbons bright.

Keep watch! Take stock. Call out the hours till light.
With voice thin but sweet I hum against the night.

At the Monastery

Three months I have been here
the days beginning to look one
much like the rest. Alone I sit
staring out window, notebook askew
in lap, pen on floor. With nothing
to distract me I distract myself
trailing tails of thoughts jerking
and snapping from acorn cap
to acorn cap, turning each over to find
it empty. More beckon and off they
go until watching them grows tiresome.
How easy it is to do nothing
to wrap in winter fog and sleep
open-eyed the hours. Faces leer
from loaf-shaped rocks in the wall
outside my cell. I shall not
listen to their lewd mutterings
shall not worry how to explain
these hours wasted to those
I've left back home.

On My Daughter's Birthday

You slipped from me then
as you slip from me now
a blessing
a wound.

Friday of the Passion

Four crows congregate on melting lake ice
feathers quaking like black cassocks
in the wind. They're tearing the flesh
of a drowned squirrel they'd retrieved

from water's edge. Two gorge; two wait
in ritual it has taken most of the morning
to assemble amid much cawing and bowing.
When satiated they swoop away, only to return

when hungry. I fed this squirrel all winter
old rolls I found in freezer which I thawed
on kitchen counter before breaking into bits
on the low rock wall. Its companion because

not dead comes now seeking crumbs.
I also fed these crows. Nothing wasted. Nothing
meaningless. Body of life given for you.
I take another roll from the freezer.

Offertory Hymn

With my face to its rising, sun
    shatters fog
grasping at lowlands, and cobwebs
sagging from dew are
    suddenly bejeweled. For a moment
    I forget where I've been where
I'm going. Bell rings. I turn from glass
toward day blessed with
    its share of busy boredom. Later

on my knees
    next to student's chair I lay
out my halting questions probing
memory scabbed yet seeping, stuttered
    incarnation, gaps cabalistic, mind
    unfathomed and unfathomable.
Beauty, such beauty I gaze
too long when doubt and fear
    pass back between us, the butter and

bread together
    we must eat along with
knowledge, this inheritance. What have I
to give except the I behind? who am I to take? My
    own disappointments vying with theirs, dreams
    shatter and surge. In a windowless office
down the corridor I lay words flat
praying they rise from page and
    like shell strangling yolk-smeared chick

let me break.

Easter Dinner

The daughters-in-law begrudge their husbands' freedom
to escape the kitchen. They carefully tend everything
that simmers—ham gravy, brown-sugar kissed beans,
resurrected slights—bringing all to the table. Grace said,
awkward and stumbling since but a holiday occurrence,
the grandsons grab for more than their share,
granddaughters served second, if at all. Red eggs tell
of pickling with beets, not of risen truth, no Magdalene
recognized here among the pressed linens, although
the aunts mutter against the short skirt of a pretty niece.
Potato filling goes round once, twice, the dish so hot
it can't be passed easily, so one spoons for another.
Elbows bump, hands touch. Someone jumps up
to get the forgotten butter, jam. Grandchildren vie
to taste each pie: cherry, shoo fly, berry custard,
apple, coconut cream, mincemeat, peach. Greasy plates
stacked on the counter, crumbs strewn over the white
cloth, they sit, sated, loath to begin the washing, and speak
of absent ones, too much rain, fields yet to till, sprouting
garden plants on windowsill. They look at each other,
rolled open by grins, grudges mere shrouds draped on rock;
then eyes move away, embarrassed. Wrapped closed
once again, the women stand to run the sudsy water.

Quilted Lamentation

One day a year after he shot himself, I picked
through remnants in my chest, browns dark
as sodden clods, fat quarters of red like coagulated

blood, some bone, a bit of fire-scorched maize.
The second day I cut, fabric puckering slightly
as the blade slipped through a blur of color,

my fingers smoothing the way before it. Next I pieced
blocks of triangles, light with dark, the machine humming
words hammered by father, repeated by son:

Bitch. Brainwashed. Stupid. Cow. I watched
the needle fall and rise, punch holes in fabric,
and wondered if they released my anger

or stitched it tight to scorch through long winters
ahead like some cloak cursed. Days passed like this,
long chains of blocks spilling off table to be cut

apart, seams pressed to one side, tails trimmed.
I forgot to feel. Then one day I, too, went down
on floor to arrange and re-arrange blocks

until design emerged. He did it on my birthday,
after all, his death to me as his life, a present
of hate-ugly scraps. I bound up the edges.

The Inland Sea

Every July we make the long journey east to sleep in her attic,
the bed floating amidst cast-off furniture, two portholes tucked
under eaves open to what little breeze may come, grimy curtains
becalmed. I stare up at the bowed rafters as we pitch through waves
of anger, my husband asleep.

Down below, she unravels the mistakes of the day from the afghan
she's crocheting, her failing eyes misreading the pattern yet again,
as she waits the return of all she's lost. Her husband wanders still
in the land of mind-eating lotus; her son enticed by siren song of land
so black it grows dreams.

Her grandson sleeping above with me will not stay, driven away
by her nagging. She keeps the photo of him stuck in the frame
of the living room mirror. He stands in short white pants, bow tie
clipped to his shirt, king of her stoop, belly stuck out, ever a child
caught by the spell of celluloid.

Like any good huswif, she equates love with a table loaded—
homemade noodles and chicken falling from bone, pepper slaw,
chow chow, coconut cream pie—yet fretted to neighbors this evening
about the effort demanded to feed me, the stranger who is wooing
her grandson from her.

In some versions the son kills the father unknown. But in this one,
he kills himself, leaving the old man to grow fat and lazy in his chair,
unwashed, unshaven, sometimes rousing himself to pee in the front yard.
It is the grandson's fate to journey further inland where no one
knows the coils of the Schuylkill.

In all versions, the wife loses as she gains: those she does not love
press her; those she does, doubt her while she holds vigil
in the marriage bed, now mouldering. Men she knew by touch
and smell change so she knows them no longer, replaced by
murderers of her dreams.

She and I are one in that at least. Unable to find rest

in that stuffy attic, I close my eyes and walk through rooms of memory—
hers or mine?—carrying a smoking branch of hyssop, waiting
for the meddlesome gods to stop
the vengeance in my heart.

Pruning Lesson

Avoid allegory, I tell them at the seminary, for
this generation needs parable, not to make sense

of their world but to turn it upside down. So why
do I keep staring at this bonsai, a Juniper stunted

by patient shearing to look like what it is not—
an ancient tree wind-scoured on some rocky cliff.

Avoid the beginner's mistakes, the nurseryman
tells me, of overwatering and pruning roots

at the wrong time, and don't protect it indoors.
Pick one with many branches so you have choices

for removal. You have a head start if you
select one with dead branches and scars;

otherwise you'll have to create them. He tells
me what I already know. Would it, I wonder

be just as beautiful if allowed to grow
unhindered. But I already know that, too.

What You Fail to Bring Out of You

Shadows will get you in the end
the prim will spout obscenities
the geezer drop his pants and bend
to leering time's senility.

Nothing denied completely flags
no thing overwhelmed stays tethered tight
like fermenting yeast in airless casks
rages grow stronger lacking light.

Do you the dying walk among graves
harboring bits of each buried there
until they rip from shriveled frames
like spores burst from pod into air.

Ode to Anger

Bitch, shrew, comeuppance that's due:
you've played me fair
and demand what's owed.

Nag, scold, dark shadow gone cold:
bank your embers
deep so never flag.

Fiend, bag, wild banshee unclad:
strip away fear
that love cannot breach.

Crone, witch, twin-lipped sucking leech:
your potions too
sweet turn acrid, parch.

Frump, tart, she-wolf big with art:
tease and tip me
debauched by your buss.

Brat, chit, wild-eyed puking puss:
tuck here at my
breast and I'll rock you.

Prayer for the Heart II

If true that weeds are plants but out of place
then must misaimed love be diligently
also uprooted, thrown on compost space
to starve sun-scorched in a world of plenty.

Still for years I could never tell pigweed
from carrot, earthy want from deep desire,
till roots entwined—one orange, one red—
and I'd damage the true expunging liar.

Only late do I find within me endures
an indiscriminate heart which ever lusts
after the dross as well as what's pure
delighting when wild phlox invades iris.

Flesh-robing God, among us yet apart,
indulge for now the weeds seeding my heart.

Gift of the Aloe

Like her mother-in-law before
the tongue sharpens as her husband's
arm weakens. I turn from closed door

bearing her gifts in silence stunned.
A marriage long enduring but
long disappointing can shift ground

between, I know, push up what's buried
or seed more of same in families
of ragged shoots. A balm, anger,

on freezer burns of resentment
but one must break for one to find
a healing salve. What cracks within

me what kind of mother will I
be to daughter's husband? Enough.
I throw out her bitter melon

sort her cast-offs for charity
but set the plant on window sill
near stove and nearer still to heart.

Consider the Spider

From eaves above the window where I write
she dangles, demonstrates what can be done
with what spins out of one. Her aerial feats
occur without a net which they create
in fact, defying sense, defying heart, she
leaps, falls, hangs mid-flight—a moment ticks
with doubt? with fear?—then drops, no outstretched hand
to catch her fall save she herself, else drift
on breeze. She brings up short, climbs back to eave
and leaps again. Again. Shape manifests.
Yet she if not to be ensnared by her
own trap must its filaments cut clean through
with scissor-laced legs as she runs the length
demanding old with stuff of self make new.

Daughter of Abraham

The story always ends with a crowd-pleasing scene:
some memorable words, bit of spit and mud, then hush
of anticipation before the snap of spine
straightened, the loud suck of breath in one done, the shriek
of demons fleeing into swine. Quite a show, that.

What they don't tell is how those freed stepped back in lives
defined by bonds: did she confront spouse who'd bent her
down with burdens too heavy; did the child survive
the suffocating care of parents scared to lose
again; did he forgive kin who'd chained him naked
with the dead? A less spectacular story, that.

No wonder many begged to follow him, skip town,
the mess of reconciling left behind.
Impossible to claim a daughter's fortune from
that lot yet impossible to stay the same once
awakened. Better to ignore dilemma, chase
after wonders incomplete since empty of work,
covenants without cost, story lacking caveat.

At the Beginning Word

Why do you call yourself
a farmwife, the professor asked
her voice betraying judgment,
but because I chose to hear
only curiosity I tried to answer.

In the end my tongue tied.

How explain to a nomad grazing
her postings that I am wedded to field
and man, season and crop,
that freedom is slavery unless
I can name where I am bound.

In the beginning we are all bound.

On Driving Past Walden Pond, Massachusetts

What can I say: it changed everything.
Not the place, of course, the book

which spoke metaphor to confusion. When he
said to hoe one's beans I left studying

sea and things of deep for farmer's flatland
and planted beans: Top Crop and Jade,

Tenderette and Henderson Bush, green,
yellow, waxy and smooth. I learned

which are best for fresh eating
and which for canning. I learned

seedling from weed, how to look for
beetle eggs on underside of leaf. I learned

to bed limas with sand so monstrous cotyledons
do not break their crooked necks emerging.

What I did not learn was how to admit
I took him at his word, confused tenor

with vehicle, had nothing to show for years
of hoeing but pantry of jarred beans.

Four decades later come to choose again
I find I'm once more on the road to Pond

so near to sea. This time belted
to seat forewarned of his siren call

I steer on past leaving past another
narrative to tell and song filling ears

turn the wheel by inland stars for home
and rolling fields of beans.

Inner Garden Green

Not sure if it's malice or heedless boredom but
every year I lose something to their carelessness.
The tractor's wide tracks grind off an edge

or a swing of the boom curls raspberry
leaves yellow, nubbins of what would
have become berries left hanging

like nearly decapitated heads clinging
to their thorny spines. Or a fly-away rebar
skewers melons to a straw stuffed bed.

Their own gardens are sporadically tended.
If pole beans fail, they know someone else
will have an extra bucket to replace those lost.

They do not offer what I have lost. I think
of this as I stand in the hardware store
picking out grass seed, fescue perhaps

or Kentucky blue. I imagine a green arc
two mower rounds wide as buffer for garden
from field. Inside sage fills a central plot

ringed by spinach, cabbage. Next a patch
of dill to repel mites, beets dusky as a family bible,
berries red and black. Lavender will tumble

near trellises sagging under abundantly
loaded peas. Maybe some mint in buried pots
to keep it from getting out of hand, a few chives

for snipping into soups. But what to do
with pumpkins? Their ruddy chambered meat
and rapacious vines will efface scribed rows.

At the margins they must go to scramble

through my husband's corn—I see no better
way—and all things until harvest risk.

Small Town Minds

Someone poisoned my neighbors: broke
their well casing and poured fine granules
of arsenic down the deep chamber. Disaster
undetected in each cup of tea, forkful
of boiled spaghetti, sip at the faucet
to flush foamy toothpaste.
Lucky, the doctor said.

He struggles still with symptoms; she
lay in hospital for weeks. But the
dosage was not lethal for adults.
If their grandson had visited then,
there'd have been another funeral for
me to play, up on the organ bench
in the balcony, a small coffin at the altar below.

Cops have no leads, it seems, no motive,
no suspects, but we suspect. Too large
he was: too outspoken for confined livestock,
too competitive at land auctions, their home
a squire's mansion ringed by iron, gardens
of weeping cherry and statuary—not
beans and potatoes—leaded glass.

Sunday I stand with neighbors—a poet
among butchers, farmers, truckers,
clerks—and grab their offered hands of peace,
wondering which it was that fouled that well,
that drove them to the city, unwilling to live
in that house, this community.
Small town, small minds, they say.

I suppose they're right. This town is small.
I eat the bread, take the cup from the
neighbor standing before me, and as the red
liquid approaches my lips, bread granules
floating on its surface, I wonder

if my mind is too small to see or too large
to feel the poison accumulating in us all. I drink.

Cicada Song

In days of light, I trill of light
    and darkness.
In years of dark, I pray to dark
    and light.

I dwell in dank and climb to sky
    for why I can't explain:
great hungers prey in gut and loins,
    compel from me such strain.

Please show your face this day I chirr,
    Beloved.
A change I sense will world again
    inter.

Still silence shrouds your heart from me;
    pray do your wings beat near?
Until that moment we embrace
    I trill a way to clear.

Potato Harvest

For where your treasure is, there also will your heart be. Mt 6:21

Sunday after the liturgy, after the meal
after we've taken Mother home, my husband
and I dig potatoes.

Some prefer a fork, but in our clayish
soil, we find a spade works best
to turn the hills that baked all summer.

The September sun at our backs, we begin
with the Red Pontiacs. He places shovel close
to avoid digging barren ground but not so close

to slice flesh. He lifts slightly and the shovel
reveals a trove of red-skinned beauties. I brush
the soil away like some anthropologist, and cradle

them careful not to scratch the papery skins, then
drop them in a five-gallon pail. He
turns the blade to dig again.

We bow to the rows stretching east to west—one
of these Reds for roasting, dusted with rosemary
and garlic; two of Kennebecs for frying and baking

in their jackets; and last the Yukon Golds,
their mashed yellow flesh destined
for the Thanksgiving table.

My mother-in-law is right: digging
potatoes is like digging for treasure and
this year the line of pails extends along the garden's edge.

My back aches and I kneel, jeans a thin barrier
from the clods. A line from the morning's gospel
crawls through my mind as I crawl after the shovel.

We slip into a rhythm of minimal motion, each
anticipating where the other will be. His body
bends towards mine and from a distance, we must look as one.

The Tongue Has No Bone

When I tell you I love you I believe
it's true. This spineless muscle savors all
my words the same. Perhaps I've merely fused
love's taste with salty lobes my tongue licks clean
when whispering to you. Everything
is as it is: that Christmas you gave a
thesaurus after I refused at first
your ring. It sat for years untouched, maligned
mute testament to words flung out in pain
to cause more pain intended or no. This
too I believed—until just meter grasped
and turned all out inside to tales our tongues
branded on bone. Could you see what I could
not, that words would bring me back to you.

Susan Yanos has been a lay ecclesial minister, professor of writing and literature, and director of college writing programs, including the Ministry of Writing Program at Earlham School of Religion, Richmond, Indiana. She holds degrees in biology, literature, and pastoral theology and is a certified spiritual director. She is the author of *Woman, You Are Free: A Spirituality for Women in Luke*, and co-editor and co-author of *Emerging from the Vineyard: Essays by Lay Ecclesial Ministers*. Her poems, essays, and articles have appeared in several journals; her article on Indiana's literary history is included in the *Dictionary of Midwestern Literature*, Volume Two. Currently retired from university teaching, she serves as a spiritual director, retreat leader, and free-lance editor. She lives with her husband on their farm in east central Indiana where she tends to her hens, fruit trees, and gardens.

CPSIA information can be obtained
at www.ICGtesting.com
Printed in the USA
BVHW041431250219
541104BV00010B/243/P

9 781635 348477